Yy

Kelly Doudna

Published by SandCastle™, an imprint of ABDO Publishing Company, 4940 Viking Drive, Edina, Minnesota 55435.

Printed in the United States.

Cover and interior photo credits: Artville, Digital Stock, Eyewire, PhotoDisc, Stockbyte

Library of Congress Cataloging-in-Publication Data

Doudna, Kelly, 1963-
    Yy / Kelly Doudna.
       p. cm. -- (The alphabet)
    ISBN 1-57765-445-5
    1. Readers (Primary) [1. Readers] I. Title.

PE1119 .D6869 2001
428.1--dc21

00-056903

The SandCastle concept, content, and reading method have been reviewed and approved by a national advisory board including literacy specialists, librarians, elementary school teachers, early childhood education professionals, and parents.

Let Us Know

After reading the book, SandCastle would like you to tell us your stories about reading. What is your favorite page? Was there something hard that you needed help with? Share the ups and downs of learning to read. We want to hear from you! To get posted on the ABDO Publishing Company Web site, send us email at:

sandcastle@abdopub.com

Revised Edition 2002

About SandCastle™
Nonfiction books for the beginning reader

- Basic concepts of phonics are incorporated with integrated language methods of reading instruction. Most words are short, and phrases, letter sounds, and word sounds are repeated.

- Readability is determined by the number of words in each sentence, the number of characters in each word, and word lists based on curriculum frameworks.

- Full-color photography reinforces word meanings and concepts.

- "Words I Can Read" list at the end of each book teaches basic elements of grammar, helps the reader recognize the words in the text, and builds vocabulary.

- Reading levels are indicated by the number of flags on the castle.

Look for more SandCastle books in these three reading levels:

Level 1 (one flag)	**Level 2** (two flags)	**Level 3** (three flags)
Grades Pre-K to K 5 or fewer words per page	**Grades K to 1** 5 to 10 words per page	**Grades 1 to 2** 10 to 15 words per page

Yvonne has fun with her dog.

Yestin grows taller each year.

Yetta likes to yell.

Yuki wears a yellow top.

Yul swings in the yard.

Yuli makes yummy snacks.

Yulia is five years old.

Yoselin has a younger brother.

Where does Yancy play?

(yard)

Words I Can Read

Nouns

A noun is a person, place, or thing

brother (BRUHTH-ur) p. 19
dog (DOG) p. 5
fun (FUHN) p. 5
snacks (SNAKS) p. 15
top (TOP) p. 11
yard (YARD) pp. 13, 21
year (YIHR) p. 7
years (YIHRZ) p. 17

Proper Nouns

A proper noun is the name
of a person, place, or thing

Yancy (YAN-see) p. 21
Yestin (YEST-in) p. 7
Yetta (YET-uh) p. 9
Yoselin (YOHZ-uh-lin) p. 19

Verbs

A verb is an action or being word

More Yy Words

egg yolk

yarn

yawn

yo-yo